ASTHMA ATTACK

By Charis Mather

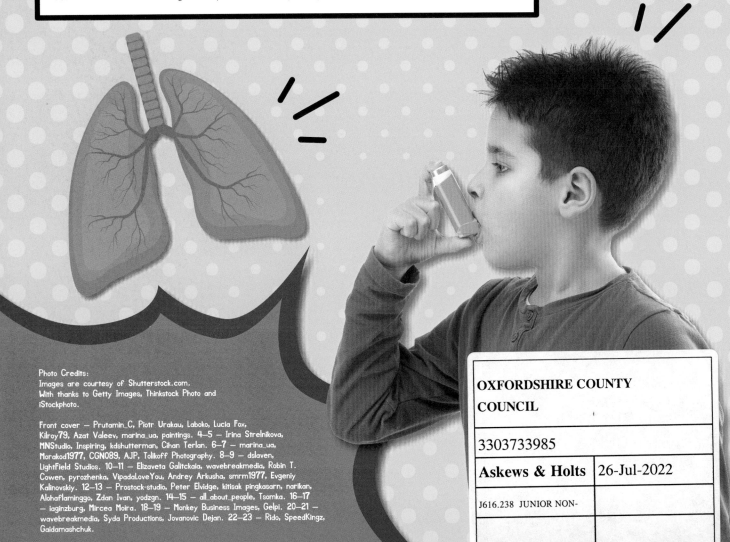

BookLife
PUBLISHING

©2022
BookLife Publishing Ltd.
King's Lynn, Norfolk
PE30 4LS, UK

All rights reserved.
Printed in Poland.

A catalogue record for this
book is available from the
British Library.

ISBN: 978-1-80155-629-3

Written by:
Charis Mather

Edited by:
Robin Twiddy

Designed by:
Jasmine Pointer

*All facts, statistics, web addresses and URLs in this book were verified as valid and accurate at time of writing.
No responsibility for any changes to external websites or references can be accepted by either the author or publisher.*

*The contents of this book are intended as solely informative and should not be considered medical advice.
BookLife recommends contacting medical professionals for specific guidance.*

Photo Credits:
Images are courtesy of Shutterstock.com.
With thanks to Getty Images, Thinkstock Photo and
iStockphoto.

Front cover — Prutamin_C, Piotr Urakau, Laboko, Lucia Fox,
Kilroy79, Azat Valeev, marina_ua, paintings. 4–5 — Irina Strelnikova,
MNStudio, Inspiring, kdshutterman, Cihan Terlan. 6–7 — marina_ua,
Morakod1977, CGN089, AJP, Tolikoff Photography. 8–9 — dslaven,
LightField Studios. 10–11 — Elizaveta Galitckaia, wavebreakmedia, Robin T.
Cowen, pyrozhenka, VipadaLoveYou, Andrey Arkusha, smrm1977, Evgeniy
Kalinovskiy. 12–13 — Prostock-studio, Peter Elvidge, kitisak pingkasarn, narikan,
Alohaflaminggo, Zdan Ivan, yodzgn. 14–15 — all_about_people, Tsomka. 16–17
— iaginzburg, Mircea Moira. 18–19 — Monkey Business Images, Gelpi. 20–21 —
wavebreakmedia, Syda Productions, Jovanovic Dejan. 22–23 — Rido, SpeedKingz,
Gaidamashchuk.

CONTENTS

PAGE 4   Would You Know What to Do?

PAGE 6   What Is Asthma?

PAGE 8   Inhalers

PAGE 10 What Are Asthma Triggers?

PAGE 12 Asthma Attack

PAGE 14 What Can You Do?

PAGE 16 Getting Help

PAGE 18 What Next?

PAGE 20 How We Feel

PAGE 22 Living with Asthma

PAGE 24 Glossary and Index

Words that look like this can be found in the glossary on page 24.

WOULD YOU KNOW WHAT TO DO?

Hello! My name is Sam. I am going to help you learn what to do in an emergency. An emergency is when something dangerous is happening. Sometimes our friends need help, so we should know what to do.

Would you know what to do in an emergency?

Lots of children and grown-ups have asthma. Sometimes people with asthma can have an emergency. Knowing what to do in an emergency means that we can help our friends.

WHAT IS ASTHMA?

Asthma is a <u>condition</u> that sometimes makes it difficult to breathe. The tubes in our body called airways bring air to our <u>lungs</u>. People with asthma have airways that can get narrower and fill with <u>mucus</u>.

This is a blocked airway.

This is a clear airway.

Most of the time, you cannot tell if someone has asthma, but sometimes someone with serious asthma might...

... feel tightness in their chest.

... cough a lot.

... make <u>wheezing</u> sounds.

... find it hard to breathe.

INHALERS

People with asthma can use a <u>reliever</u> inhaler to help them breathe. An inhaler has <u>medicine</u> inside that helps the airways to relax. You might see someone breathing in the medicine from an inhaler.

Medicine canister

Inhaler

Cap

Mouthpiece

A reliever inhaler is useful when someone's asthma gets worse. If they have a tight chest or are breathing quickly, wheezing or coughing, then it is a good idea to use an inhaler.

My inhaler has a spacer that makes it easier to use.

Spacer

WHAT ARE ASTHMA TRIGGERS?

Some things can cause asthma to get worse. These are called triggers. Triggers are things that can <u>irritate</u> the airways. Different people can have different triggers.

People with asthma have to be careful around these triggers.

Smoke

Sprays

Dust

Cold air

Pollen

Animal fur

Exercise

These are some common asthma triggers.

ASTHMA ATTACK

During an asthma attack, the airways close so much that it is hard for air to get in or out of the lungs. Attacks can happen very suddenly or slowly get worse over a few days.

Asthma attacks often happen at night.

During an asthma attack, someone might...

... wheeze or cough a lot.

... feel tightness in their chest.

... not be able to talk.

... start breathing very quickly.

... find an inhaler is not helping.

Someone who is having a very serious asthma attack might not make any noise. Their fingers or lips might look blue.

WHAT CAN YOU DO?

Many people with asthma have inhalers. They have been shown how to use one in emergencies. Different inhalers may give different amounts of medicine.

Always listen to what your doctor says about using an inhaler.

Asthma attacks can be scary. Make sure that you stay calm and help your friend stay calm. You should call for help if someone is having an asthma attack.

If there is no adult nearby, you can call emergency services.

GETTING  HELP

Emergency services are people who are <u>trained</u> to help during an emergency. If you call about an asthma attack, they will tell you what to do. Sometimes they send people to help.

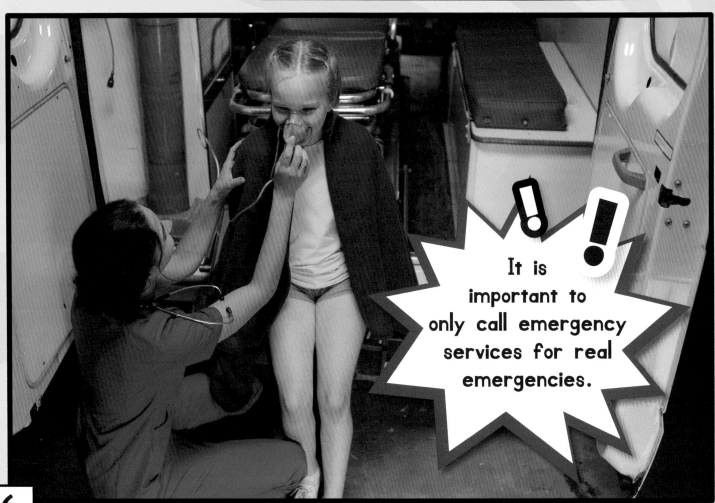

It is important to only call emergency services for real emergencies.

Do you know the emergency phone number where you live? Ask a grown-up to show you how to call emergency services.

Emergency services might ask these questions:

What is your emergency?

What service do you need?

What address are you at?

WHAT NEXT? ??

It is important for someone to tell their doctor if they have had an asthma attack or are worried about their breathing. Doctors can help us know what to do next.

A doctor might help someone learn about their triggers.

HOW WE FEEL

Emergencies can cause us to have lots of questions. It is okay to ask questions about asthma, but we should never be unkind. Each person is different, and we all need help sometimes.

What makes you different?

Having asthma can make some parts of life more difficult. Our friends who have asthma might find this hard or upsetting. We must be kind and helpful to those people.

LIVING WITH ASTHMA

Many people grow out of their asthma when they get older. Some do not, but they can still do things they enjoy. People with asthma can learn how to manage it.

23

GLOSSARY

CANISTER	container
CONDITION	when your health is affected by something
IRRITATE	to hurt because of something on or in the body that should not be there
LUNGS	a pair of organs in your chest that are used to breathe air
MEDICINE	something used or taken to fight off illnesses or pain
MUCUS	a slimy material, such as snot, found in some parts of the body
POLLEN	yellow powder released from some plants that gets carried by the wind
RELIEVER	medicine that is used to help relax the airways
TRAINED	having been shown how to do something properly
WHEEZING	breathing with a whistling or gasping sound when the airways are narrow

INDEX

AIRWAYS 6, 8, 10, 12
DUST 11
EMERGENCY SERVICES 15–17
EXERCISE 11
FUR 11
INHALERS 8–9, 13–14, 19, 23
LUNGS 6, 12
MEDICINE 8, 14
POLLEN 11
SMOKE 11
SPRAYS 11
TRIGGERS 10–11, 18–19